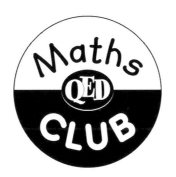

Maths QED CLUB

Using Numbers Book 2

Ann Montague-Smith

64

23

QED Publishing

QED

Written by Ann Montague-Smith
Designed and edited by The Complete Works
Illustrated by Peter Lawson
Photography by Steve Lumb

Publisher Steve Evans
Creative Director Louise Morley
Editorial Manager Jean Coppendale

Printed and bound in China

Now try this

Say all the numbers
from 0 to 100. Now count
backwards, starting with
100, 99, 98...

100, 99,
98, 97, 96,
95, 94...

50

62 63 64 ⬤ ⬤ **67** ⬤

79 ⬤ ⬤ ⬤ ⬤ **84**

⬤ **90** ⬤ ⬤ **93** ⬤

95 ⬤ ⬤ **98** ⬤ **100**

7

Counting to 100

The dogs have spilt paint on the number strips.
Can you work out which numbers are missing?

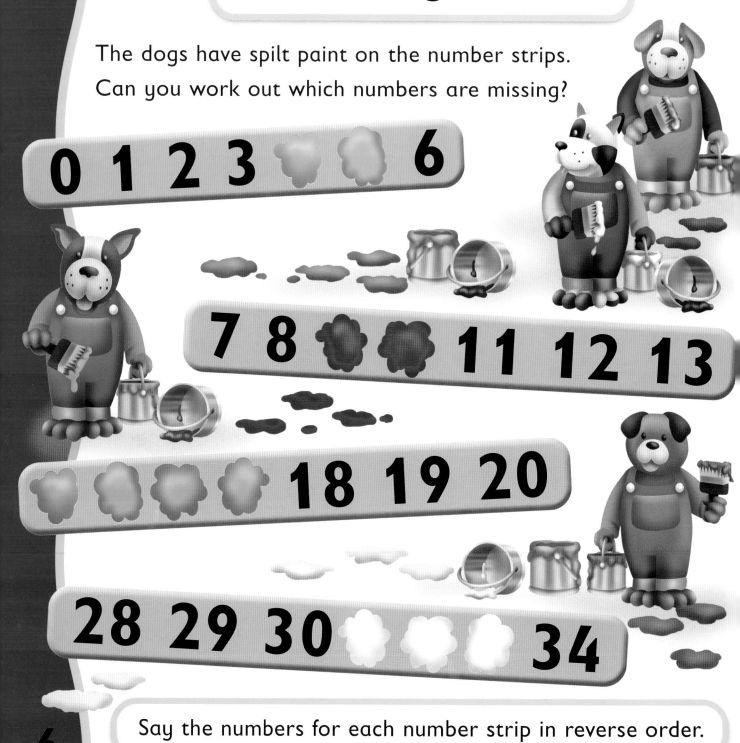

0 1 2 3 ▮ ▮ 6

7 8 ▮ ▮ 11 12 13

▮ ▮ ▮ ▮ 18 19 20

28 29 30 ▮ ▮ ▮ 34

Say the numbers for each number strip in reverse order.

6

1 2 3 4

Try this

With a friend, take turns to say a number between 1 and 99. Now decide whether to count up to 100 from that number, or down to 0. Now write that number, and the next nine numbers, in order.

Start at 45 and count back.

62 63 64 65

66 67 68 69

70 71 72 73

74 75 76 77

78 79 80 81

82 83 84 85

86 87 88 89

90 91 92 93

94 95 96 97

98 99 100

Finish 5

You also use your teeth when you speak, especially your front teeth. For example, try to say the word 'teeth' without touching your front teeth with your tongue.

Your teeth help you to make 'hard' sounds like 't' and 'd'.

Activity

Use a mirror to check your teeth. How many do you have? Do you have any gaps?

Different shapes of teeth

You have three kinds of teeth. The front teeth have a wide, sharp edge, and are called incisors. You use them like a knife to slice through food.

Your front teeth are sharp and strong.

6

Behind your front teeth are four sharp canine teeth. You use your canine teeth to tear off mouthfuls of food.

The teeth at the back of your mouth are called molars. You use them for chewing.

Molar   Incisor   Canine

Teeth have different shapes so you can bite and chew food.

Activity

Put a piece of cracker between two spoons. Crush the cracker between the spoons. This is how your molars grind up food.

Two sets of teeth

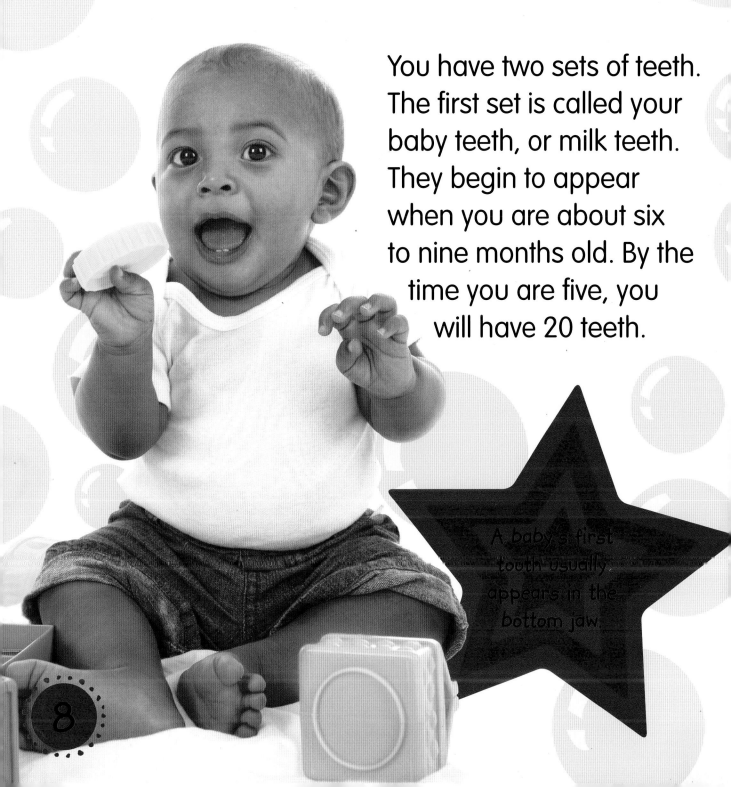

You have two sets of teeth. The first set is called your baby teeth, or milk teeth. They begin to appear when you are about six to nine months old. By the time you are five, you will have 20 teeth.

A baby's first tooth usually appears in the bottom jaw.

8

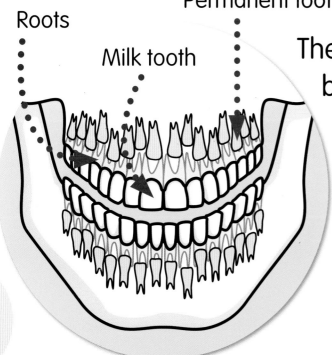

Roots

Permanent tooth

Milk tooth

Each milk tooth has a permanent tooth growing below it.

The second set of teeth grow below the milk teeth. They are called permanent or adult teeth, and there are 32 of them.

As each permanent tooth grows bigger, it pushes the milk tooth above it. This loosens the milk tooth until it falls out.

Activity

When a milk tooth falls out, examine it closely. Can you see any root? Compare its size to an adult tooth.

Inside a tooth

A tooth has three layers. The outer layer of **enamel** is the hardest thing in your body. The **dentine** below is as strong as bone. The centre is filled with soft **pulp** that contains blood vessels and nerves.

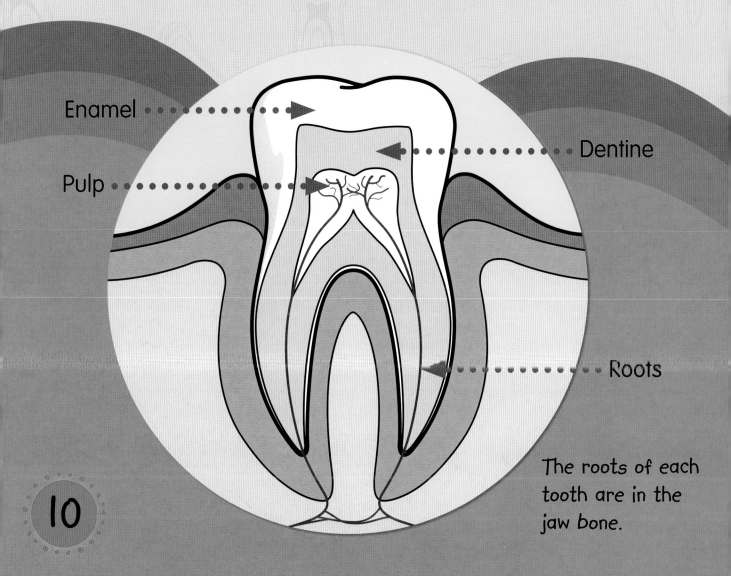

Enamel

Dentine

Pulp

Roots

The roots of each tooth are in the jaw bone.

Acid can damage your teeth by making a hole in the enamel. The hole is called **tooth decay**.

A small hole in a tooth is called a cavity.

Activity

Put a whole uncooked egg in a glass, cover it with vinegar, and leave it overnight. Vinegar is an acid. It takes the **calcium** out of the eggshell in the same way that acid in your mouth attacks your teeth. In the morning, the eggshell will be soft.

What causes tooth decay?

Your mouth contains germs called bacteria. They are too small to see, but they feed on sugar left in your mouth. As they feed, they make **plaque**.

Plaque contains acid, which can cause tooth decay. Plaque and bacteria can also affect your gums. They may make your gums bleed.

When tooth decay causes a hole or cavity, it can be very painful. Children and adults can suffer from tooth decay.

12

Dentists can treat tooth decay. They drill away the rotten part of the tooth and fill the hole. This is called a filling.

When a dentist fills a tooth, it stops decaying.

Activity

Find a large potato with one or more 'eyes' in it. With adult help, dig out the eyes with a potato peeler. Put a teaspoon of icing sugar into a bowl and add two drops of water. Use the mixture to fill the holes, like a dentist fills teeth.

13

cleaning your teeth

Cleaning your teeth brushes away sugar and plaque. You should clean your teeth when you get up and before you go to bed. If possible, you should also clean them after meals.

Try to clean your teeth after eating anything sweet.

14

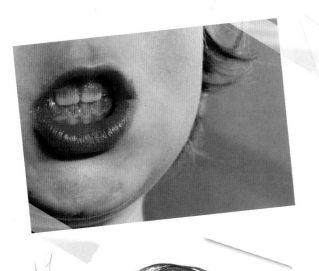

Activity

Disclosing tablets show how well you have brushed your teeth. When you suck one, it colours the plaque red or purple. Clean your teeth again until all the colour has gone.

Always brush from your gums to the tips of your teeth. Brush the back of each tooth as well as the front, and remember to clean the tops of your molars, as well as your gums.

15

Sugar damages your teeth

Fizzy drink

Doughnuts

Sweets

Sweet food and drinks are bad for your teeth. Fizzy drinks, cakes, biscuits, sweets and chocolate all contain lots of sugar. When you have swallowed them, some of the sugar stays in your mouth and can cause tooth decay.

Biscuits

Cake

These are just some of the foods and drinks that contain sugar.

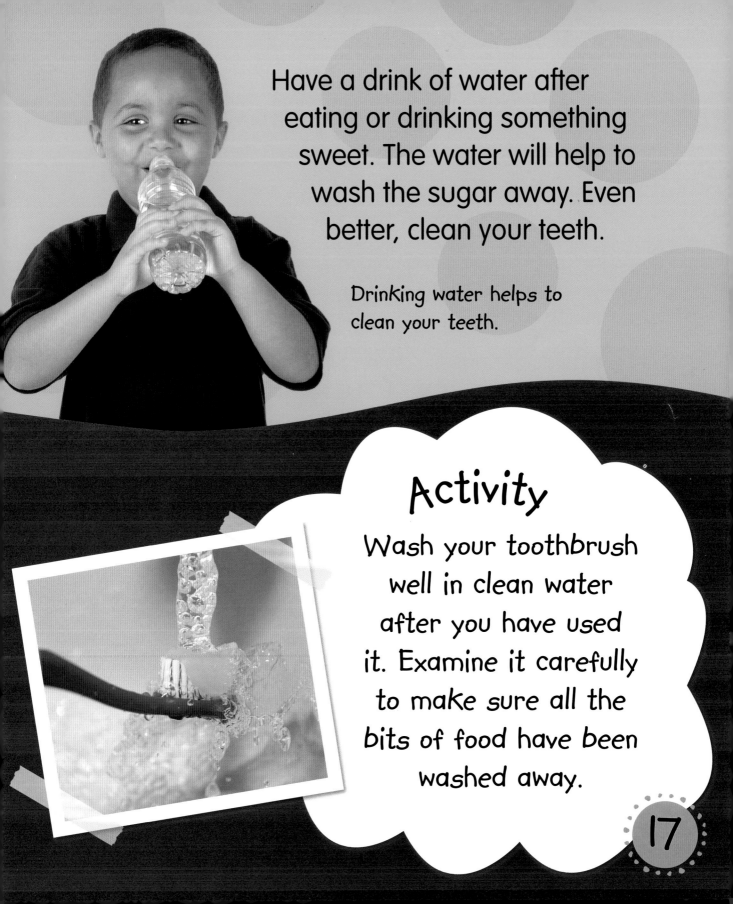

Have a drink of water after eating or drinking something sweet. The water will help to wash the sugar away. Even better, clean your teeth.

Drinking water helps to clean your teeth.

Activity

Wash your toothbrush well in clean water after you have used it. Examine it carefully to make sure all the bits of food have been washed away.

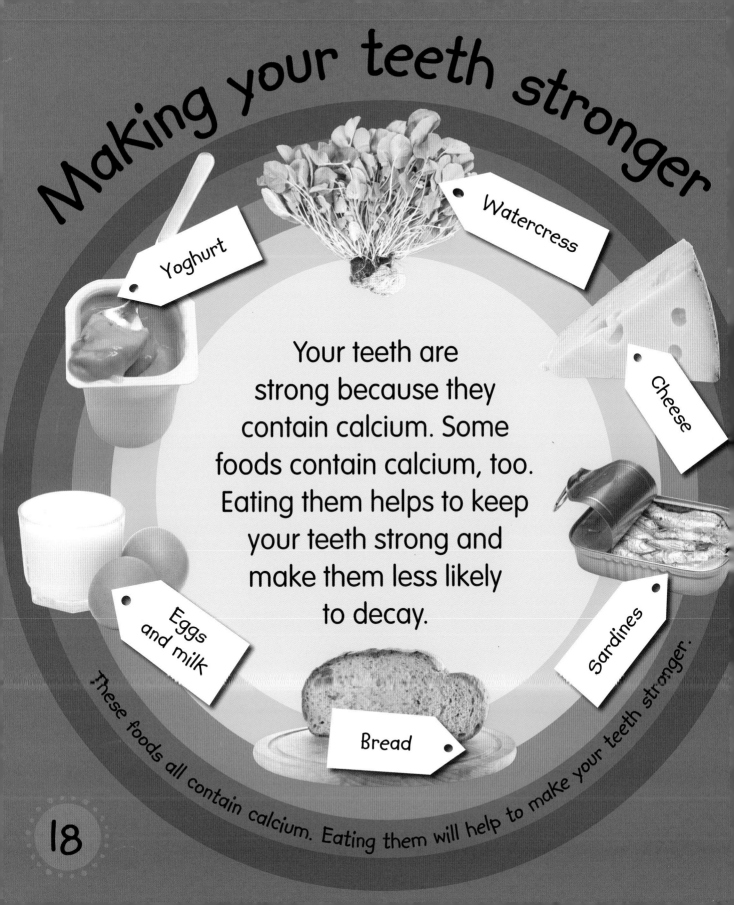

Making your teeth stronger

Yoghurt

Watercress

Cheese

Your teeth are strong because they contain calcium. Some foods contain calcium, too. Eating them helps to keep your teeth strong and make them less likely to decay.

Eggs and milk

Sardines

Bread

These foods all contain calcium. Eating them will help to make your teeth stronger.

18

Fluoride makes the enamel on your teeth stronger. Most types of toothpaste contain fluoride, and, in some places, fluoride is also added to tap water.

Try not to swallow the toothpaste. If you often have too much fluoride, it can discolour your teeth.

Activity

Make a healthy, calcium-filled lunch. You could start with a cheese, ham and salad sandwich. Then you could eat a yoghurt or an orange.

19

Going to the dentist

You should have a dental check-up every six months. The dentist looks at all your teeth to see if you have any tooth decay. The dentist also checks that your adult teeth are growing well.

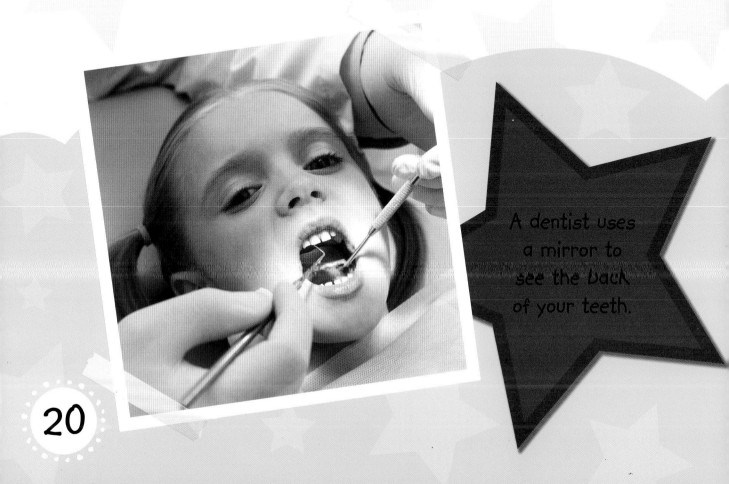

A dentist uses a mirror to see the back of your teeth.

You may sometimes get toothache in one of your teeth. It might be caused by eating something very cold. If you have toothache that does not go away, you should go to the dentist.

Cold food can make your teeth hurt, but just for a moment.

New

Old

Activity

Check your toothbrush to make sure the bristles are straight and firm. If they are not, you need a new toothbrush.

Glossary

Calcium
The substance that makes your teeth and bones hard and strong. Some foods also contain calcium, such as cheese and milk.

Dentine
The main part of a tooth is made of dentine. It is similar to bone and is covered with a layer of very hard enamel.

Enamel
The hard, glossy outer layer of a tooth. Enamel contains calcium and fluoride. It is the strongest substance in the body.

Fluoride
One of the substances that makes the enamel and dentine in your teeth strong. Most toothpastes contain fluoride.

Plaque
A sticky substance that is made by bacteria in your mouth. Plaque contains acid that can cause tooth decay. Cleaning your teeth helps to remove plaque and stop it forming.

Pulp
This is the soft material in the centre of a tooth. It includes blood vessels and nerves.

Tooth decay
A tooth decays when part of it rots. Tooth decay begins when acid in the mouth eats a hole in the enamel of a tooth. If it spreads to the soft pulp in the centre of the tooth, it can be very painful.

Notes for parents and teachers

1. Talk to the children about how cleaning their teeth helps to prevent tooth decay.

2. Search the Internet to find diagrams of a full set of milk teeth and a full set of permanent teeth. Count the teeth and see which extra teeth are included in the permanent teeth. Copy the plans of the teeth and help your child to colour in the milk teeth that they have already lost, and the permanent teeth that have already come through. Some families leave money from the 'Tooth Fairy' under a child's pillow whenever a milk tooth falls out.

3. Talk about tooth decay and the foods that contribute to it. Make a list of drinks and foods, particularly treats, that contain a lot of refined sugar. Discuss how you can limit the intake of these foods to once or twice a day, and how drinking water after having them or, better still, cleaning their teeth, helps to prevent tooth decay.

4. Encourage the children to suck a disclosing tablet after they have cleaned their teeth. Do the same yourself and compare how well you and the children have cleaned your teeth.

5. Take your child for a dental check up every six months. Set an example by having your own teeth checked at the same time.

23

Index

Numbers to 100

Play this game with a friend. Take turns to throw a small coin onto the spinner. Move your counter that number, on the windows of the buildings. Say the number you land on out loud.

Start

1 2 3 4

5 6 7 8

9 10 11 12

13 14 15 16

17 18 19 20

21 22

23 24 25

26 27 28

29 30 31

32 33 34

35 36 37

38 39 40 41

42 43 44 45

46 47 48 49

50 51 52 53

54 55 56 57

58 59

60 61

Take turns to point to any number.
Ask your friend to say it.

4

Contents

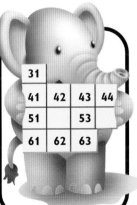

Tens and units

Match the tens and units balloons to the items of food.

83 **17** **62** **50** **30** **36** **19**

10 lollipops
10 lollipops
10 lollipops
10 lollipops
10 lollipops
10 lollipops
10 lollipops

10 sweets
10 sweets
10 sweets

10 chocolates

Which is the largest tens and units number?
Which is the smallest?

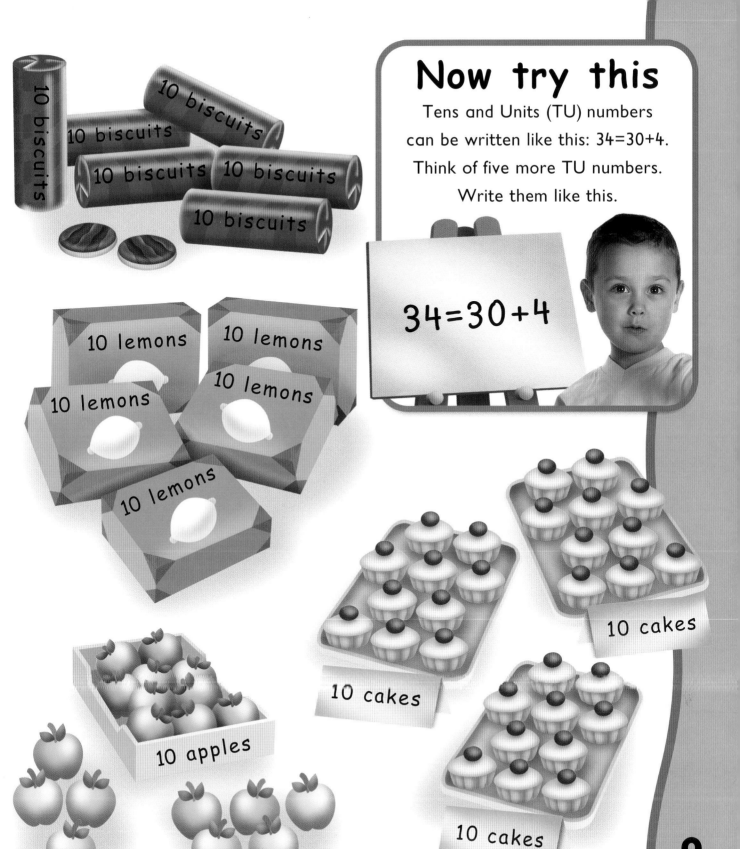

10 biscuits
10 biscuits
10 biscuits
10 biscuits
10 biscuits
10 biscuits

10 lemons
10 lemons
10 lemons
10 lemons
10 lemons

10 cakes
10 cakes
10 cakes
10 cakes

10 apples

Now try this

Tens and Units (TU) numbers can be written like this: 34=30+4. Think of five more TU numbers. Write them like this.

34=30+4

9

Counting on or back

Choose a number from the carpet below. Count on from that number to 100, then back again.

1	2	3	4	5
11	12	13	14	15
21	22	23	24	25
31	32	33	34	35
41	42	43	44	45
51	52	53	54	55
61	62	63	64	65
71	72	73	74	75
81	82	83	84	85
91	92	93	94	95

Choose some more numbers and do it again.

6	7	8	9	10
16	17	18	19	20
26	27	28	29	30
36	37	38	39	40
46	47	48	49	50
56	57	58	59	60
66	67	68	69	70
76	77	78	79	80
86	87	88	89	90
96	97	98	99	100

Ordering numbers to 100

Some of the t-shirts have lost their numbers.
Look at the numbers on the ground.
Which numbers will fit in the spaces on the t-shirts?

6   **16**

56

55   **67**   **1**   **46**   **15**

12

Which number will not fit? Can you explain why?

Try this

You will need some playing cards.
Take out the picture cards.
Take 2 cards. Make a TU number
with them. Now make another
TU number with your cards.
Write as many numbers as
you can that will fit between
your 2 numbers.

29

37

41

84

22

60

5

73

49

18

50

More or less

Read the numbers on the labels. Say the number that is 1 more than each number. Now say the number that is 1 less than each number.

Do this again. This time say the 10 more and 10 less numbers.

14

Challenge

Write down any number between 30 and 80. Now write down the number that is 20 more. Write down the number that is 20 less. Now write all your numbers in order, starting with the smallest number.

18 38 58

51

36

72

48

87

15

Missing numbers

Some of the numbers have fallen off this piece of a hundred square that Gerry Giraffe is holding. Which ones?

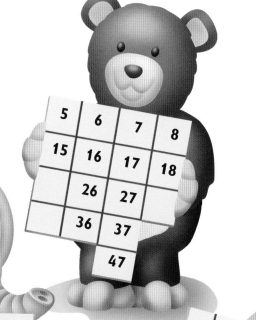

Now look at the pieces of the hundred square the other animals are holding. Work out which numbers are missing.

16

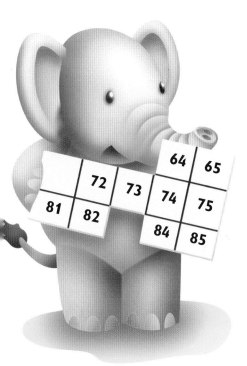

			64	65
	72	73	74	75
81	82			
			84	85

Now try this

Mark with a pencil a 10 by 10 grid on some squared paper. Write 1 in the top left-hand corner square, and 100 in the bottom-right hand corner square. Take turns to write in any number on the grid until all the numbers from 1 to 100 are there in order.

1	2	3	4	5	6	7	8	9	10
11	12	13	14	15	16	17	18	19	20
21	22	23	24	25	26	27	28	29	30
31	32	33	34	35	36	37	38	39	40
41	42	43	44	45	46	47	48	49	50
51	52	53	54	55	56	57	58	59	60
61	62	63	64	65	66	67	68	69	70
71	72	73	74	75	76	77	78	79	80
81	82	83	84	85	86	87	88	89	90
91	92	93	94	95	96	97	98	99	100

45	46		
55	56	57	58
	66	67	68
		77	78
		87	88

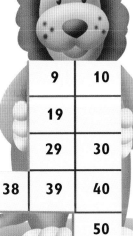

	9	10
	19	
	29	30
38	39	40
		50

48	49	
	59	
	69	70
		80
	89	90
98	99	100

17

Rounding

Numbers with units from 1 to 4 round down to the nearest 10. Numbers with units from 5 to 9 round up to the nearest 10. Round the numbers on the apples.

86

75

6

31

91

47

36

43

99   98

Write all the numbers on the apples in order. Write underneath the number that each apple number will round to.

Now try this

This girl wants to buy 35 sweets to share with the children in her class. The sweets come in packs of 10. How many packs of sweets must she buy? Suppose there were 32 children in her class. How many packs of sweets would she need now? Explain your answer to a friend.

82

57

14

65

78

43

19

24

92

84

19

Path problem

The numbers on the path must be painted on. The first slab reads '1'. The last slab will read '99', so this will need two 9s to be painted. How many number 1s need to be painted? How many number 2s, 3s, 4s, 5s, 6s, 7s, 8s and 9s?

Can you find a quick way to work this out?

21

Supporting notes

Numbers to 100 – pages 4–5

Encourage children to read the numbers and to write them. Point to any number and check that the children can read it. If they are unsure, discuss the tens number, then the units number, then the whole number, so that the child begins to understand how the number is made up.

Counting to 100 – pages 6–7

If children are unsure about numbers larger than about 30, count together from 0 to 100 and back again, several times. Now point to the numbers on the page and read these together, so that children become more confident with the numbers before tackling the task.

Tens and units – pages 8–9

As well as being able to read and write tens and units numbers, children need to understand what each of the digits stand for. If children are unsure about this, read the tens and units numbers in two ways. For example, take 25: 2 tens and 5 units is the same as twenty-five.

Counting on or back – pages 10–11

If children are unsure about counting to 100, then they can make mistakes such as twenty-nine, twenty-ten, twenty-eleven. Check that the children understand what to say at the decade change: 29, 30… 39, 40… and so on.

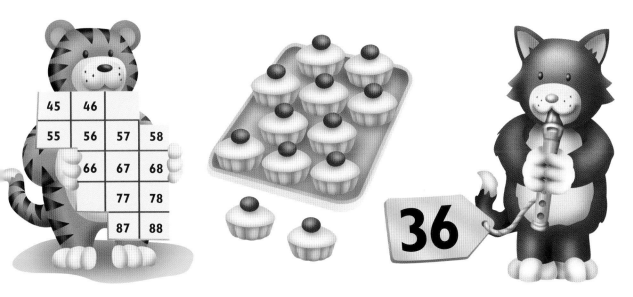

Ordering numbers to 100 – pages 12–13

If children are unsure about which numbers could fit in the spaces, count on from the smaller number to the larger number. This will help children to realise which numbers could fit.

More or less – pages 14–15

If children find this activity difficult, ask them to write out the numbers from 1 to 100, or do this for them, in a grid with 1-10 along the first line, 11-20 along the next and so on, lining up the numbers. Use this to find the 1 more and 1 less numbers, then the 10 more and 10 less numbers. Ask 'What do you notice about 10 more? And 10 less? Where do these come on the grid?'

Missing numbers – pages 16–17

Children may find it easier to tackle this activity with a full hundred square grid, with 1 in the top left-hand corner, and 100 in the bottom right-hand corner. When they are confident with using this, ask them to try the activity again, this time without the hundred square grid.

Rounding – pages 18–19

As long as children understand the convention that units of 5-9 round up, and 1-4 round down, rounding is easy. If children do find it difficult, suggest that they write the numbers 1 to 9 in order, and draw a line between 4 and 5. They can use their line to help them remember which numbers round up, and which down.

Path problem – pages 20–21

Twenty of each of 1, 2, 3…9 will be needed. Discourage children from just counting each digit. Instead, suggest that they look at the numbers 1-9, then 11-20, then 21-30, to see how many of each digit is used. Encourage them to predict from what they notice about the overall total for each digit.

Using this book

The illustrations in this book are bright, cheerful and colourful, and are designed to capture children's interest. Sit somewhere comfortable together as you look at the book. Children of this age will normally be able to read most of the instructional words. Help with the reading where necessary, so that all children can take part in the activities, regardless of how fluent they are at reading at this point in time.

The activities in this book will extend children's knowledge about numbers, from numbers to 30, to numbers up to 100. Children will begin to understand how individual digits combine to make a number, such as 3 and 5 can make 35, and can also make 53. What matters is where each digit is placed, and whether it is in the tens or units position. If children are unsure about this, do give more help with reading numbers. For example, use a pack of cards with the digits 0 to 9. Ask the children to take two cards and make a TU (tens and units) number, such as 45 with a 4 and a 5 card. Ask them to read the number. Now ask them to reverse the digits and to say what number they have now: 54. This could become a game, where one child shows a TU number, and another child says the other number that could be made with the same digits.

Encourage the children to explain how they worked out the answers to the questions. Being able to explain their thinking, and to use the correct mathematical vocabulary, helps the children to clarify in their minds what they have just done. Also, where there are children who are not so sure of how to solve the problem, hearing what others did, and how they did it, helps them to use these methods more effectively.

Do encourage children to make notes as they work at an activity. They can record numbers, writing them in order, or write simple sentences to explain what they did. Encourage them to be systematic in the way that they work, so that they do not miss a vital part of the evidence that they need to find a solution.

Above all, enjoy together the mathematical games, activities and challenges in this book!